900L

Cornerstones of Freedom

Thurgood Marshall and the Supreme Court

Deborah Kent

CHILDREN'S PRESS®
A Division of Grolier Publishing
New York • London • Hong Kong • Sydney
Danbury, Connecticut

Library of Congress Cataloging-in-Publication Data

Kent, Deborah.
Thurgood Marshall and the Supreme Court / by Deborah Kent.
    p. cm.—(Cornerstones of freedom)
    Includes index.
    Summary: Narrates the life of the first African-American to
serve as a judge on the United States Supreme Court.
    ISBN 0-516-20297-9 (lib.bdg.)   0-516-26139-8 (pbk.)
    1. Marshall, Thurgood, 1908–1993—Juvenile literature. 2. Afro-
American lawyers—United States—Biography—Juvenile literature.
3. Afro-American judges—United States—Biography—Juvenile
literature. [1. Marshall, Thurgood, 1908–1993. 2. Lawyers.
3. Judges. 4. Afro-Americans—Biography.] I. Title. II. Series.
KF8745.M34K46 1997
347.73`2634—dc20
[B]
[347.3073534]
[B]   96-9865
                                                           CIP
                                                            AC

In the summer of 1951, Oliver Brown tried to enroll his eight-year-old daughter, Linda, in school. One school was twenty blocks from the Browns' house. To walk there, Linda would have to cross a railroad track. Another school was an easy walk from where the Browns lived. The choice seemed clear. But Linda could not enroll in the school nearer to her home. It was for white children only, and Linda Brown was African-American.

Eight-year-old Linda Brown was not allowed to enroll in a Topeka, Kansas, school for white children.

Thurgood Marshall

School segregation was legal in the United States, as long as students were given equal facilities.

In 1951, many states had laws that strictly segregated (separated) students according to race. One such state was Kansas, where the Browns lived. When Oliver Brown could not register his daughter in the school of his choice, he went to court and sued the Topeka, Kansas, Board of Education. As a Kansas taxpayer, Brown argued, he should have the right to send his daughter to any public school. After three years, the case went before the United States Supreme Court, the nation's highest judicial body. This landmark case is known as *Brown v. Board of Education of Topeka.* To present his case, Brown had a dynamic African-American lawyer named Thurgood Marshall.

A white woman barred the way as black youths attempted to be seated at a segregated lunch counter in Memphis, Tennessee, in 1961.

Marshall knew the humiliation of racial segregation. When he traveled in the southern states, he had to stay at hotels reserved for black patrons. He could not enter restaurants with signs that read "Whites Only." Restrooms, drinking fountains, waiting rooms, telephone booths, hospitals, and even cemeteries were segregated.

Thurgood Marshall believed that the most painful form of segregation occurred in public schools. From the time they entered kindergarten, most children in all-black schools received a lower quality of education than many white children received.

The United States Constitution was written in 1787.

The Fourteenth Amendment to the United States Constitution guarantees "equal protection of the law" to all citizens. But the courts in each state can interpret the Constitution in different ways. Late in the 1800s, the Supreme Court ruled that a state could maintain "separate but equal" facilities for blacks and whites. Separate schools for black children were lawful, as long as they were equal in quality to the schools for white students.

Arguing the case of *Brown v. Board of Education of Topeka,* Thurgood Marshall stood before the nine black-robed judges of the Supreme Court. He demonstrated that the southern states spent nearly twice as much money on the schools for white students as they did on the schools for black students. He called several teachers and psychologists as witnesses. These witnesses claimed that segregated schools gave black children poor self-esteem. Marshall concluded by arguing that a separate school system could not give "equal protection of the law" to African-Americans.

On May 17, 1954, the Supreme Court announced its decision on *Brown v. Board of Education.* Spectators and reporters packed the court's chambers in Washington, D.C., to hear the verdict.

Chief Justice Earl Warren read the court's conclusion aloud. "To separate [black children] from others . . . solely because of their race generates a feeling of inferiority," he began. "We conclude that in the field of public education the doctrine of 'separate but equal' has no place. Separate educational facilities are inherently unequal." The decision was unanimous. All nine Supreme Court justices agreed that segregated schools violated the U.S. Constitution.

Thurgood Marshall and all African-Americans won a great victory. With *Brown v. Board of Education,* American law made a powerful commitment to ensure equality for black citizens. In the years that followed, segregated schools, hotels, drinking fountains, and lunch counters gradually disappeared. In the battle against the nation's segregation laws, Thurgood Marshall was a leading warrior.

Chief Justice Earl Warren

Thurgood Marshall (center) celebrates with fellow lawyers on the steps of the Supreme Court following the court's unanimous decision that school segregation is unconstitutional.

Thurgood Marshall was born on July 2, 1908, in Baltimore, Maryland. One of his grandfathers served in the Union Army during the United States Civil War. A great-grandfather was a slave; the Marshall family claimed he was so defiant that his master was forced to set him free.

Thurgood Marshall grew up in a racially mixed neighborhood. Whites and blacks lived side by side. But Maryland maintained a segregated school system. Thurgood could not attend school with the white children who lived in his neighborhood.

Thurgood was a superior student, but he tended to argue with his teachers. His elementary-school principal had an unusual way of punishing children who talked back to their teachers. He sent them to the school basement and would not let them return to class until they memorized long sections of the U.S. Constitution. Years later, Marshall commented wryly, "Before I left that school, I knew the entire Constitution by heart."

Thurgood's mother and father tried to shield their children from the effects of racism. But they also taught their children to defend themselves. "Once I heard a kid call a Jewish boy I knew a 'kike' to his face," Marshall once recounted. "I was about seven. I asked him [the Jewish boy] why he didn't fight the kid. He asked me what would I do if someone called me

Thurgood Marshall (top row, second from right) at Lincoln University

'nigger.' Would I fight?" Marshall asked his father what he should do if he were ever insulted by racial slurs. His father replied sternly, "Anyone calls you 'nigger' you've not only got my permission to fight him—you've got my orders to fight him."

Thurgood Marshall's father worked as a waiter in a railroad dining car. He had little education, but he taught his son how to debate. Marshall often remarked that his father taught him how to argue. Marshall also commented, "[Father] never told me to become a lawyer, but he turned me into one."

In 1925, Thurgood Marshall graduated from high school and entered Lincoln University in Oxford, Pennsylvania. To help meet expenses, Thurgood worked part-time as a cook and a busboy at a local restaurant. Cooking became his lifelong hobby.

Movie theaters had separate entrances and seating areas for whites and blacks.

Lincoln University was an all-black school, and the town of Oxford was segregated. One night, Marshall and five friends walked downtown to attend a movie. After they bought their tickets, they made an important decision. They wanted to sit on the first floor, where the white patrons sat, instead of climbing to the balcony, where blacks were required to sit. After they took their seats, an usher pleaded with them to move to the balcony. But the students refused. Eventually, the usher gave up. After the movie, the students walked triumphantly out of the theater. "We desegregated the theater in the little town of Oxford," Marshall said later. "I guess that's what started the whole thing [Marshall's desire to end discrimination] in my life."

Lincoln University was an all-male institution, but Thurgood met girls at church services. One

Sunday he met Vivian Burey, a student at the University of Pennsylvania. They fell in love and were married when they were both twenty-one years old.

After he graduated from Lincoln, Thurgood Marshall applied to the University of Maryland Law School. He was turned down because he was black. Never in its history had the school accepted an African-American student. At the time, the standard of "separate but equal" was firmly in place. But the University of Maryland Law School was the only tax-supported law academy in the state. Marshall argued that Maryland failed to provide blacks with even the "separate but equal" facilities demanded by the law. Nevertheless, school officials would not yield.

Instead, Marshall enrolled at Howard University, the famous mostly black college in Washington, D.C. One of his law professors at Howard was Charles Hamilton Houston. Houston had a profound impact upon young Marshall's life. He encouraged his students to use the legal profession to fight racist laws. Houston was also a humanitarian. He saw the law as a means of improving the lives of all Americans, not only those of African descent. Under Houston's guidance, Marshall had come to see the law as a tool that could transform the country. He hoped to specialize in civil-rights cases and to break down the barriers of a segregated society.

Charles Hamilton Houston

ONE WORLD – OR NONE

Thurgood Marshall encouraged African-Americans to demand equal civil rights.

Marshall graduated from Howard University with honors in 1933. He returned to Baltimore, rented a tiny downtown office, and opened his own law practice. As a lawyer, he was determined to serve the city's poor people. Unfortunately, most poor clients could not pay their legal fees, but Marshall never turned anyone away. Though he worked long hours, his business struggled. He paid his assistant only $7.50 a week. He had to borrow a rug from his mother's house to put on the office floor. At the end of his first year in practice, Marshall was $1,000 in debt. Still, he continued his work.

In 1935, Marshall accepted the case of a black student named Donald Murray. Like Marshall, Murray had been rejected by the University of Maryland Law School on the basis of race. After hearing the case, a Maryland judge ordered the University's law program to accept Murray as a student. Marshall won this important case, and Murray was the first black student ever admitted to a state-run law school located anywhere south of the Mason-Dixon line.

Soon after that victory, Marshall joined the legal staff of the National Association for the Advancement of Colored People (NAACP). Founded in 1909, the organization worked to end discrimination against African-Americans. At the NAACP, Marshall was reunited with his Howard University law professor, Charles Houston.

Marshall worked tirelessly as a lawyer at the NAACP.

As a result of Thurgood Marshall's work at the NAACP, he quickly became a leader among African-American lawyers. One of his memorable victories came in Dallas, Texas, in 1938, where he secured the right of black citizens to be chosen as trial jurors.

In 1939, Marshall argued his first case before the U.S. Supreme Court. Arguing a case before the nation's highest court is often the crowning achievement of a lawyer's career. During his long career as an attorney, Marshall argued thirty-two cases before the Supreme Court. Twenty-nine of these cases were decided in his favor. By 1954, when he argued *Brown v. Board*

The United States Supreme Court, Washington, D.C.

of Education of Topeka, Thurgood Marshall was one of the most famous lawyers in the United States.

Despite his success in the courtroom, Marshall's personal life was touched by tragedy. In 1950, Charles Houston, his longtime mentor, died of a heart attack. Friends remarked that Marshall grieved as if he had lost a father. Then, in 1955, Marshall's wife Vivian died of cancer on her forty-fourth birthday. For months she had concealed her illness from her husband, fearing the news would interfere with his work. When Marshall finally learned of her condition, he put his work aside to care for her. Rarely leaving their New York City apartment, he cooked meals and tended to her every need. When Vivian died, he told a friend that he felt as if the world had come to an end.

A year after Vivian's death, Marshall married Cecelia Suyat, a former assistant at the NAACP. The couple eventually had two sons.

Cecilia Suyat Marshall (center), with the Marshalls' two sons, Thurgood Jr. (left) and John (right)

Martin Luther King Jr.

After he remarried, Marshall threw himself back into his work. The 1950s and 1960s were an era of upheaval that brought the collapse of lawful segregation. A civil-rights movement arose in Montgomery, Alabama, in 1955. One evening, a black woman named Rosa Parks refused to give up her seat to a white passenger on a city bus. Her action triggered the Montgomery bus boycott, which was led by the young minister, Dr. Martin Luther King Jr. During the year-long boycott, blacks in Montgomery refused to ride the city buses until the seating was desegregated.

In the early 1960s, thousands of civil-rights demonstrators, both black and white, poured into southern cities. They held "sit-ins" at segregated restaurants, in which they would refuse to leave an establishment until they received service. They also held "wade-ins" at segregated city pools, and "pray-ins" at segregated churches. Eventually, the movement led the U.S. Congress to pass the Civil Rights Act of 1964 and the Voting Rights Act of 1965. With the help of these new laws, legal segregation in the United States finally came to an end.

In 1960, four African-American college students sat at a lunch counter in Greensboro, North Carolina, and refused to leave until they were served (above). African-Americans demonstrated in support of civil rights outside City Hall in Albany, Georgia, in 1961 (left).

RACIAL SEGREGATION

Drinking fountains labeled "Colored" reflected the legal segregation that was common in the United States, especially in the South.

Segregation laws began in the United States in the early 1800s. These laws required that whites and blacks use separate public facilities. Segregation was most prominent in southern states, where blacks suffered severe discrimination. In the 1930s, laws began to be passed to eliminate segregation. But the 1950s and 1960s are remembered as years of social upheaval throughout the South, as blacks and whites struggled with the issues of racial equality and desegregation.

IN THE UNITED STATES

Policemen arrested this woman because she tried to enter a rest room reserved for white women only.

Even African-Americans who served in the United States military had to endure racial segregation.

In 1961, President John F. Kennedy offered Thurgood Marshall a position as a federal judge. The appointment meant that Marshall would have to leave the legal staff of the NAACP. Despite his deep attachment to the organization, he decided to accept the new job. In a 1965 interview, he claimed that he accepted the judgeship because he had achieved his goals in the area of civil rights.

Thurgood Marshall was sworn in as a federal judge on October 3, 1961.

Marshall served as a federal judge for four years. In 1965, President Lyndon Johnson named him solicitor general, the third-highest position in the U.S. Department of Justice. When Marshall accepted the appointment, Attorney General Nicholas Katzenbach called him "one of the greatest Americans alive today." As solicitor general, Marshall represented the U.S. government in court. He argued in favor of current American law. This pro-government stand was a dramatic change for a man who had previously been dedicated to fighting against existing laws. But by the time

Thurgood Marshall and his family following his appointment as solicitor general of the United States

Marshall was named solicitor general, laws in the United States had changed drastically. The Civil Rights Act and the Voting Rights Act were tools to transform the country by providing equal rights to all citizens.

In June 1967, President Johnson nominated Thurgood Marshall to a seat on the U.S. Supreme Court. Only a few years earlier, such a nomination would have shocked most Americans. No African-American had ever served on the highest court in the nation. But the civil-rights movement had broadened public attitudes about racial issues. Thurgood Marshall was considered to be exceptionally qualified for the job of Supreme Court Justice.

Justice Tom C. Clark

When Marshall took his seat on the court, he replaced Justice Tom C. Clark, who retired. Clark came from an old southern family. Newspaper columnists noted that Clark, the grandson of a Confederate soldier, was being replaced by Marshall, the great-grandson of a slave.

The Supreme Court has nine judges, called justices. Cases are decided on a majority basis.

When considering a case, the justices refer to the U.S. Constitution, a document written more than two centuries ago. The Constitution is often called "the supreme law of the land." It presents the rules to be followed by the government and by individual Americans. The primary task of the U.S. Supreme Court is to bring the spirit of the Constitution into modern life. The Supreme Court is one of the most powerful bodies within the government. Even Congress and the nation's president must abide by its decisions.

President Lyndon Johnson announced the appointment of Thurgood Marshall to the U.S. Supreme Court on June 13, 1967.

Justice Thurgood Marshall saw the Constitution as a set of rules that should change with the times. He often pointed out that the United States was a very different society in 1787, when the Constitutional Convention met in Philadelphia, Pennsylvania, to write the

In 1986, near the end of Marshall's career, the nine justices of the Supreme Court posed for this official photograph. Front row, from left: Thurgood Marshall, William Brennan, Chief Justice William H. Rehnquist, Byron R. White, Harry A. Blackmun. Second row, from left: Sandra Day O'Connor, Lewis F. Powell Jr., John Paul Stevens, Antonin Scalia.

Constitution. At that time, one of every five Americans was a slave, and lawbreakers were commonly hanged for such offenses as horse stealing. "I do not believe the Constitution was forever 'fixed' at the Philadelphia convention," Marshall once said. "Nor do I find the wisdom, foresight, and sense of justice exhibited by the framers particularly profound. On the contrary, the government they devised was defective from the start, requiring several amendments, a civil war, and momentous social transformation to attain the system of constitutional government . . . we hold as fundamental today."

The Constitutional Convention met in Philadelphia in 1787.

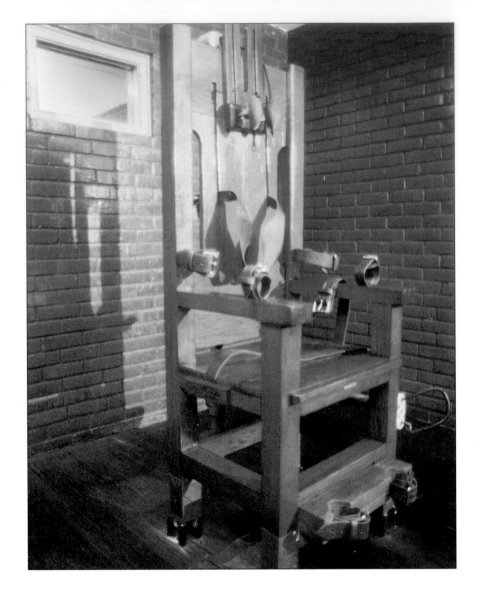

When Marshall first joined the Supreme Court, the majority of the justices shared many of his views. Marshall opposed the death penalty on the grounds that it was a "cruel and unusual punishment." Cruel and unusual punishments are forbidden by the Constitution. The other justices of the Supreme Court of the late 1960s held the same opinion. As a result, the high court often struck down death-penalty laws written by individual state governments. But the fear of violent crime became an important social issue in the 1970s and 1980s. Presidents Richard Nixon and Ronald Reagan were both elected after they

Presidents Richard Nixon (1969–1974) (left) and Ronald Reagan (1981–1988) (below) were elected after vowing to inflict harsh penalties on violent criminals.

vowed to punish criminals with harsh measures. Presidents often appoint Supreme Court justices who share their views. Marshall eventually realized that he was in the minority on cases involving death-penalty issues, or the rights of people accused of committing violent crimes.

By the late 1980s, Marshall's health was failing. He had suffered several heart attacks and a serious bout with pneumonia. News commentators began to suggest it was time for him to retire. But Marshall believed that if he retired, President George Bush would replace him with a conservative justice. Steadfastly, he refused to retire, despite his ongoing medical problems.

In 1990, a reporter asked him when or if he planned to step down from the Supreme Court. "I have a lifetime appointment [on the court], and I intend to serve it," Marshall replied.

As time passed, however, Marshall's illnesses began to affect his work. In June 1991, he

Thurgood Marshall finally announced his retirement from the Supreme Court on June 28, 1991.

Marshall's flag-draped coffin in the Great Hall of the Supreme Court

announced his retirement. He had served on the court for twenty-four years.

Thurgood Marshall died on January 24, 1993, at the age of eighty-four. His casket lay in state in the Great Hall of the Supreme Court. Some twenty thousand mourners passed through the hall to pay their respects. Throughout the country, many political leaders, judges, journalists, and ordinary citizens praised Marshall's achievements. He was honored as a man, a lawyer, and a judge. Marshall spent half his lifetime disagreeing with United States law. But he had faith that the country's sense of justice would always prevail. In 1965, at the height of the civil-rights movement, Marshall said, "I've never had to defend my country by lying about it. I can tell the truth about it and still be proud. [But] I'm not going to be completely satisfied. I'll be dead before I'm satisfied."

Thurgood Marshall is buried in Arlington National Cemetery.

GLOSSARY

conservative – traditional

demonstration

demonstration – public display of a group's feelings toward a person or cause

discrimination – practice of treating people differently, based on characteristics such as race or religion

doctrine – belief taught by a nation or church

humanitarian – person concerned with the rights and needs of all human beings

interpret – to explain the meaning (of a document, foreign words, etc.)

judicial – pertaining to justice and the court system

Mason-Dixon line – boundary line considered to be the border between the northern and the southern states

segregate

mentor – teacher or person who conveys a set of values and principles

profound – very intellectual and insightful

segregate – to separate on the basis of characteristics such as race, age, or religion

steadfast – staunch, firm

TIMELINE

Supreme Court rules "separate but 1896
equal" facilities legal

1908 *July 2:* Thurgood Marshall born

1925 Marshall enters Lincoln University

1929 Marshall marries Vivian Burey

1933 Marshall graduates from Howard University

1935 ⋯⋯ Marshall wins admission
of first black student to
Marshall argues first case 1939 University of Maryland
before Supreme Court Law School

1954 Supreme Court orders school desegregation

Montgomery bus boycott ends 1956

Marshall appointed federal judge 1961

Congress passes Civil Rights Act 1964

1965 Congress passes Voting Rights Act;
Marshall appointed solicitor general

1967

Marshall
becomes first
African- Marshall retires 1991
American on 1993 ⋯⋯
Supreme Court

January 24:
Thurgood
Marshall dies

INDEX *(Boldface page numbers indicate illustrations.)*

PHOTO CREDITS

ABOUT THE AUTHOR

Deborah Kent grew up in Little Falls, New Jersey. She received a B.A. from Oberlin College and a master's degree from Smith College School for Social Work. She spent four years as a social worker at the University Settlement House in New York City. She then moved to San Miguel de Allende in Mexico, where she wrote her first young-adult novel, *Belonging.*

Ms. Kent is the author of more than a dozen novels and numerous nonfiction titles for young readers. She lives in Chicago with her husband, children's-book author R. Conrad Stein, and their daughter, Janna.